Dog Tricks

Written by Tracy St Clair Pearce

KUDOS

Published by Kudos, an imprint of Top That! Publishing plc.

Tide Mill Way, Woodbridge, Suffolk, IP12 1AP.
www.kudosbooks.com

Contents

Introduction

This guide gives you all the basic information for training your dog, showing an easy and straightforward way of creating a fun partnership with your pet.

In this book pups from seven months to dogs of eleven-and-a-half years, of varying sizes have been used to demonstrate the trainability of any dog.

Remember the key elements of training with any animal: be firm, be fair and have fun.

In an ideal world all dogs should have access to a safe and secure garden area so they are able to run around and enjoy life.

When you obtain your new charge, whether it is a puppy or an adult dog, you should know what the breed was bred for. All terriers were bred to dig, so a spotless garden will soon have holes in it. Spaniels are flushers of game birds, meaning they have boundless energy and think nothing of charging through the bushes to find birds to wake up.

Labradors and other retrievers love to carry things around in their mouth, or just chew things when nothing else is available.

Whatever breed or cross breed you take on it should be integrated into your family, being spoken to, and involved in your daily life, as you become its pack. Immediately discourage any behaviour that is unacceptable. Your dog will then know the house rules and learn how to behave in an agreeable, social manner towards you and visitors.

All dogs should have at least one good walk a day, and puppies should have a couple of short walks. Socialisation is the foundation for having a happy pet. Right from the start of your new partnership it is essential to introduce the dog to all types of life – big people, children, traffic, other 'safe' dogs – anything that will make your charge a better pet.

Worming and Vaccinations

Any puppy bought from a breeder should have been wormed (at eight weeks old this should be done a minimum of three times to purge round worm). Similarly, adult dogs, if they come from a dog home or centre should have been wormed, but do check. If the dog came from any other source, try to establish its medical history. All dogs carry worms at some stage so once a pup is past six months old it should be wormed roughly twice a year.

Vaccinations must be completed before your puppy mixes with other dogs, and generally your vet will advise you when it's best to do this, usually at about eight then twelve weeks. Only use safe outside areas to train your puppy until it is fully vaccinated. Your garden, or any space where no infected dogs could have been, are best.

Puppy Crates

Crate training for little pups can be an acceptable way of having a puppy in a secure environment when small children are playing in the house and the puppy needs its own space.

The crate should be big enough for the dog to lay down in with bedding in it. It must always be a pleasure going in it. Give your puppy a little bowl of food or a big bone to chew, close the door for a little while and then let it out again. However, don't let it out if it starts whining, otherwise it will think that this is an acceptable way to get what it wants. Some puppies will voluntarily go into its den or crate for a sleep.

Young puppies sometimes urinate at first. Remove the soiled bedding and replace with clean bedding, until the puppy starts to control its bladder properly. Add a cotton sheet over the crate to create homely feel and also allows you to look into to the crate to make sure all is well.

Neutering and Spaying

Views on neutering dogs are varied, and often depend on the opinion of the local vet. For training purposes, neutering makes little difference.

Bitches normally come into season roughly every six months. The first season, which can be as late as one year after her birth, will be the bloodiest. During the middle of the bleeding (usually 10–12 days) she will be fertile, and walks in the presence of other dogs will be impossible. During this time, because her hormones will be running away with her, it is best to give training a miss.

If you decide to spay your bitch, you should allow her to have at least two seasons so all her female internal organs have had a chance to mature and function. Then wait three months after her last season before taking her for the operation. It is important to allow the hormones to settled back to their usual levels. For reference, each season lasts about three weeks, but it may seem longer!

For dogs, neutering them should be done before two years. As the male character is strongly influenced by testosterone you should wait until you notice three significant periods when the testosterone level increases naturally, the last period being just before two years. This will allow his mature character to develop. (In the wild it would be when he would leave to take over his own pack.)

Neutering is done to the male to calm him down, so neutering after the age of two years will not have the desired effect. Likewise, to have the operation carried out too early, say six months, will result in a permanent puppy attitude to life. This would be particularly unfortunate in a large dog, as he will have been deprived of any way to mature his character.

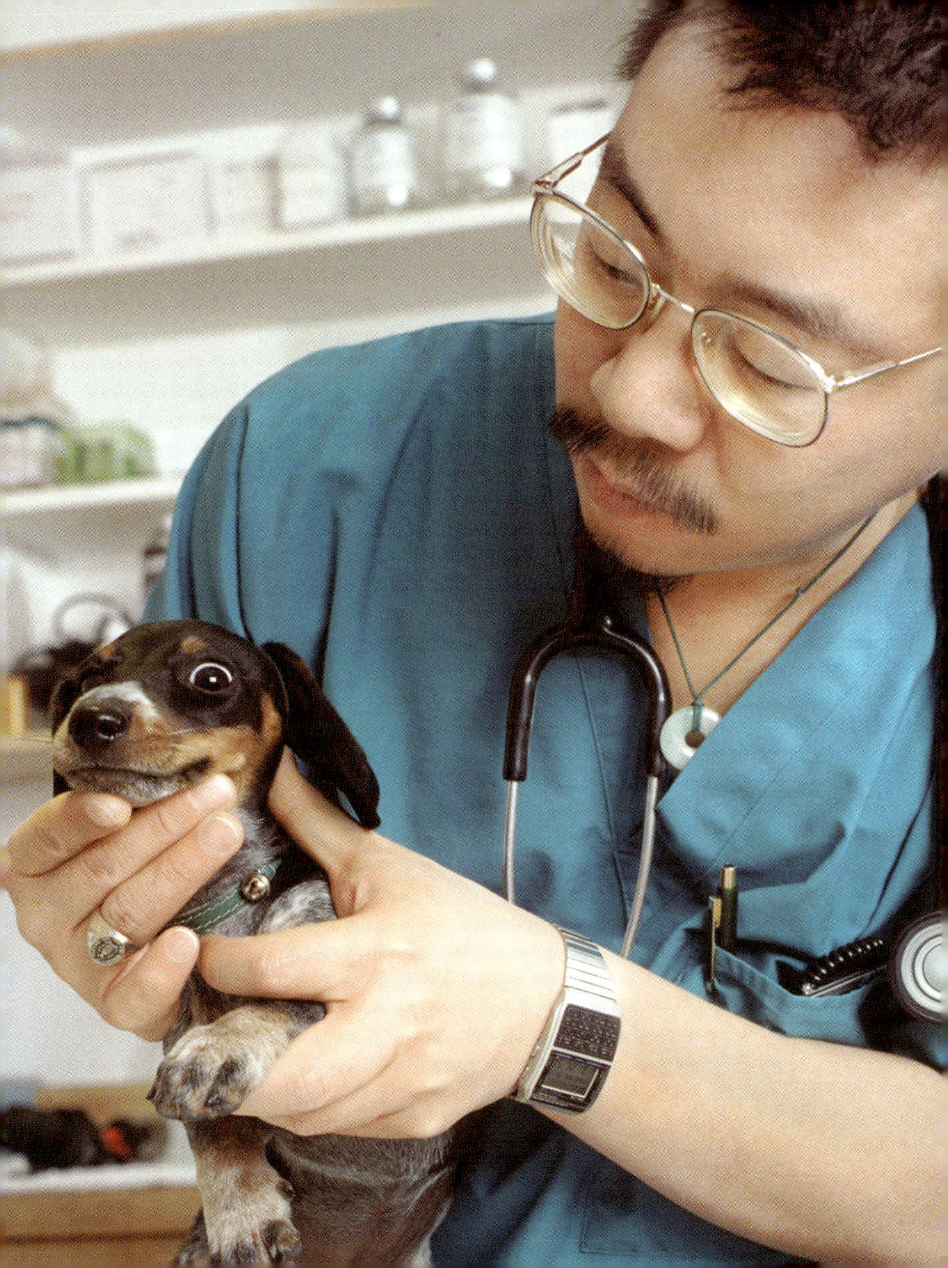

Feeding Your Dog

This is very dependent on your own views and lifestyle. For many owners, complete food, which is poured straight into the bowl and has gravy added, is a very easy option.

However, complete food can have adverse effects and your dog may produce large amounts of waste products, or have a tendency to break wind. They might need to have their teeth cleaned, especially if they are not given large bones or chew toys to keep their teeth tidy. For some breeds of dog, complete food can also cause skin conditions, so you may need to try out several varieties to find the one that best suits your dog.

Alternatively, feed your pet meat and wholemeal biscuit. Suitable meat can be beef, or lamb, lightly cooked, or chicken and turkey thoroughly cooked, with a biscuit to be added as a fibre. Grated carrot or vegetable leftovers from your own meal can also be added for fibre. You should encourage your dog to eat fish once or twice a week, particularly pilchards in tomato sauce, as the minerals and fish oils can be very beneficial.

Puppies should always come with their own diet sheet. As a guide, provide four meals a day at eight weeks, then three meals at twelve weeks, two meals at six months and one meal at twelve months. Some owners find it suits their dog to have two small meals at twelve months rather than one big meal at the end of the day. Quantities vary according to the type of food you're giving to your pet.

Remember, over-feeding your dog reduces its life and its ability to enjoy ordinary activities. A heavy-coated breed will suffer considerably in the summer if allowed to become fat.

Another important thing to remember is to never feed your dog immediately before you do any activity, which includes walking. In the summer months remember to provide plenty of clean, fresh cold water, for your dog to drink. Avoid giving too many treats during the day and monitor your dog's weight.

Simply run your hands down their flanks; in a dog of normal healthy weight you should be able to feel their ribs when you press gently against them. Seek advice from your vet if your dog seems overweight.

Only ever train your dog when you are in a good mood. It sounds simple but it is important. Your dog will sense your mood and how you feel, so leave it for another time if you seem to be having a bad day.

If possible start training your puppy or new dog the moment you get them home: titbits of meat or biscuits are excellent incentives and encourage a bond between you and your pet.

Every time you call out your dog's name, you should give them a titbit; they will come to receive the treat and will soon begin to realise they have a name to respond to. As they come to you add, 'here' to the name called: e.g. "Toby… Toby, here!" Your dog will then become accustomed to a command or action they must complete after responding to their name being called.

Your tone of voice is another aid. Use your normal tone of voice so that the command is clearly heard. Remember, dogs are sensitive to sound – a gruff voice shows displeasure, an excited tone will liven up even a bored dog.

When your dog has complied with your request, immediately give them praise. For example with the command, "Toby, sit", as soon as his bottom has touched the floor give him either his titbit or a good, gentle pat. However, they must remain seated to get the treat, so reinforce the position when necessary.

Collars and Leads

Collars and leads are the basic tools needed for an easier training relationship with your dog.

Collars

The half choke collar is the kindest and most sensible of all the training collars, as it can be used with your dog on either side of you and it will only close on your dog's neck a little way, making it easy for anyone to use.

The full choke collar is a more specialist collar that must be used correctly for it to work at all. It must be placed over the dog's head as an upside down 'P' shape just clearing their ears and sitting on their neck comfortably. When a lead is attached, the collar should run smoothly up and down the chain. It can only be used on one side as it catches on itself when you swap sides.

A common mis-use occurs when people allow their dogs to pull continually at its full length, ruining the throat region and encouraging the dog to pull.

The flat collar is only suitable for walking a well-trained dog – wide leather collars are routinely used with hounds. The down side to these collars is that they encourage pulling and your dog can easily wriggle their head out and run off, as the collar can never be tight.

ROTT

Leads

When selecting a lead, the best idea is to remember your own hands – having a chain lead in your hand will hurt, and, of course, a large chunky lead; will not be easy to hold on to. The length of the lead is also important – too short and you will be at a disadvantage, and too long you find yourself tripping over the excess.

In general, a good 1 cm leather lead or nylon lead between 1–2 metres long, which can be halved down in length for more control, is a comfortable and long-lasting solution for most dogs.

A puppy lead is always light and soft because you want to encourage your new charge to follow you happily. With puppies or any older new dog, keep their attention on you by giving titbits, pats and lots of encouragement.

Think of your lead as being a telephone line to your dog – what you are feeling will travel along it.

The Next Level

If you are interested in training your dog it will take time and patience. Take into account your own athletic ability and energy levels and your dog's own physical limitations.

Whichever group your dog comes from – whether pastoral or working, gun dogs or utility, terrier or toy – they will have different characteristics. You should realise that short-nosed breeds like pugs, bulldogs or mastiffs will find it more difficult to draw breath, so they are less suited to strenuous exercise than collies, pointers or spaniels. Also remember that large dogs such as Great Danes, Mastiffs, Newfoundlands and Wolfhounds are slow maturing and can easily be damaged by too much strenuous exercise and jumping when they are youngsters.

Terriers and toy breeds can be quite stubborn or just too delicate to risk jumping but there is no reason why, with patience, they cannot do the majority of tricks in this book. Hounds, likewise, are not at all suited to agility as they are bred to hunt by sight or by scent, but all normal control should be attainable.

Always use a common sense approach while training, and keep the health and wellbeing of your dog in mind at all times. Cross breeds should be considered and trained on an individual basis.

Dogs are normally trained on one side, usually the left. The end of the lead should be in your right hand, with the remaining length of the lead running through your left hand. Stay relaxed throughout training.

Sit

The 'sit' is the easiest position to start with. Stand in front of your dog, place a titbit in your fingers and say your dog's name. Have the titbit in front of the dog's nose. As it comes to take the item, move your hand slowly straight up. The dog will have to reach up to obtain the titbit and, in doing this it will automatically put its behind in the sitting position.

Say the word "sit" as soon as the position has been obtained, with a word of praise. If you raise a finger as you give the sit command, the dog will eventually associate the gesture with the move.

With this perfected, teach your dog to sit by your left side while on a lead. To do this still with your dog at your left knee, with both your feet and your dog's paws pointing in the same direction. Shorten the lead end in your right hand. Bring your right hand over the front of the dog's face, Bend your knees and put your left hand on the dog's lower back, placing a small amount of pressure, to obtain a clean sit. Praise your dog when the position is achieved. To release your dog from this position say "up" – a command that will be used frequently.

Stay and Wait

There are two parts to the stay command. The full instruction means the dog will not move from that position and you must go back to them to release them from the command. The second part of the stay command is 'wait', which is to hold the dog in a position (if, for example, you are going through a door and wish your dog to wait before following you). To start the stay command, place your dog in a sit position next to you, with their lead held straight up above their head in your left hand. Show the palm of your right hand to your dog as you say the words "sit" and "stay".

Count to ten, then release your dog. Increase the length of time to twenty seconds and then thirty seconds, with your dog not moving in the "sit, stay" command.

When your dog doesn't move at thirty seconds take one step away from your dog and move to the right side. This will eventually enable you to walk away from them when in the 'sit, stay' position. This command will take several attempts to achieve.

For the 'wait' command, walk as you would normally, then stop. As you stand still say "wait" to your dog holding the lead above their head to stop them moving. Count to five (this can go up to twenty as you progress) then take a step forwards releasing your dog from that command by saying "come on". Lengthening the lead as you walk starts distance control because when you say "wait" your dog will be further away from you.

Recall

The recall also has two parts to it. Firstly the 'here', which means the dog must come straight up to you, and the 'come on', which means that the dog must follow you as you are walking.

Since you have already got your dog to respond to their name before either command: "Toby, here" or "Toby, come on", you can now increase the power of the command by using an excited voice when calling your dog.

When they come to you, give a titbit and praise immediately. Do not give any other command. You may find moving backwards and clapping your hands will help keep your dog's attention with you.

To do a proper recall, sit your dog in front of you, say "wait", walk backwards, about 2.5 metres away and then call your dog: "Toby here!" Have your arms outstretched, and bring your arms in as your dog comes to you. This encourages the dog to come right up to your front. This aspect of training can be done with or without a lead. If you struggle to maintain your dog's attention then try the training again with the lead on.

Recall is another essential instruction, so you must get your dog to come to you when called before starting on the next commands.

Off

You will often have heard others say, or said it yourself, to a dog "get down" when they jump up. In truth this is an impossible command so it is little wonder the dog looks, and acts, confused.

Down means lay on the floor. If your dog jumps up at someone or onto the furniture, the correct control command is 'off'. You can add your pet's name for emphasis.

If necessary, take hold of the dog's collar and pull them off – reinforcing the command and demonstrating what the off command means.

When your dog tries to jump up at you, cross your arms and bring one knee up in front of you.

By crossing your arms you are stopping the dog getting the attention they are seeking. The raised knee, helps to push them away and reinforces the effect.

If you can turn yourself sideways – do so. This demonstrates to your dog your displeasure. You should be telling your dog "off" in a very firm manner, expressing your displeasure through your tone of voice.

Continual jumping up onto you and others is a manners and dominance problem that needs to be dealt with, especially if your pet frequently comes into contact with people outside your own family.

Heel

Heel work starts as soon as the puppy has its lead attached to its collar. By using a little titbit, toy or praise, you should encourage your pet to walk with you by your left leg. Keep the lead loose, using your voice to hold the attention of your charge.

Hold the titbit in your right hand with the end of your lead – leaving your left hand free to help. Keep your dog walking to your left side, not walking in front of you. While this is going on you should be saying "heel" to your pet.

As you advance, you can ask your dog to "watch", which means it will be looking at you continually. Remember you have to be more interesting than everything else that is going on around you. A toy or titbit will attract your dog's attention but eventually you should be able to hold their interest without props.

You must be proficient in the heel command with the lead on before starting to do this exercise off the lead. With the lead attached you have a dog you can correct and control. Off the lead you have a loose dog – a fact that will not be lost on your dog.

As you progress with heel work, corners must be managed, as well as about turns, for which there are three paces: slow, normal and fast.

Try working in a figure of eight system. This means you walk in a figure of eight on the ground, with your dog getting used to walking with you.

As you progress with your dog you will be able to square the figure of eight giving you six corners to negotiate.

Down

Ask your dog to sit next to you on your left side. Place the majority of your lead in your right hand with a little titbit. Put this hand in front of the dog's mouth, by bending over at the waist. Your left hand should be free so it can place some pressure on your dog's left shoulder area, so they are held between your left hand and your leg. With a big dog you may have to take a little step to the right as the dog goes down.

Say "down" firmly to your dog at the same time give a little pull on the lead with your right hand and drop the titbit between their paws. The left hand should be pushing gently down on the left shoulder. Praise your dog only when it has achieved the down position.

Stand up before releasing your dog with a "come on" and by taking a step away.

As your dog progresses, you will only have to say "down", dropping the sit command and you will also be able to complete the exercise without a lead.

The down command is a dominant command over a dog. Some dogs will take longer to comply than others.

Behavioural Problems

A dog may disobey a command for several reasons. It may not understand the command properly, or it may be prevented to comply by other things, or simply distracted. Sometimes, disobedience is a factor of social dominance.

With any training problem always go back to the first basic steps with the lead on.

Remember, you have to show your dog what to do. Be patient and ensure it understands what you want it to do.

You have to outsmart them. For example, a dog who surges through a door before you wants to show it is the leader of the pack. So, when you open the door, let the dog go through and then shut the door behind them, while you remain in the other room.

After a few minutes open the door again. As your dog returns to your side, slip past them and leave them in the original room. This will show them that it is your prerogative to go first and they must learn to follow.

Many problems can be solved in a similar fashion by examining the situation and learning why it is happening.

Tricks

Tricks come in handy with any dog – but they all take time to achieve and some breeds of dog are just not physically suited to some manoeuvres.

The following tricks should be taught as your dog begins to show an ability to do them, so that it only requires the correct wording and encouragement for them to comply.

Remember that you must both enjoy the lessons. An unhappy dog will turn against a command, especially if it also hurts them. That is why a soft item is used for games to start with before progressing to harder items like wooden dumbbells. To do any trick, your puppy or dog must be happy with you handling them all over and in any position. They should not resist in any manner.

As with all training, the age of the dog is significant. At six months your puppy will be able to manage up to thirty minutes of training per day. Between six and nine months forty minutes is the most advisable, and between nine and twelve months about fifty minutes. Once over a year old most dogs can cope with an hour of training as a maximum.

Remember training demands concentration from both of you. Try to plan your lesson so it is not simple repetition – mistakes are more likely to occur when your dog is bored.

Speak

When your dog starts to bark tell it to "speak" and praise it if it continues to bark. Some dogs will bark very easily, others do not have it in their nature to bark much. Sometimes when playing a game with your dog it will get excited and bark, so use these opportunities to teach it this trick.

Remember, if you encourage your dog to bark or speak you should also have a stop command, otherwise you could upset neighbours or family members. Several words can be used: stop, cease, cut or shut it. Whichever you choose it must become the command you use all the time.

In practise, say your dog's name followed by the stop command. Give it a toy or just hold its jaws together gently and calm them down. Repeat the command, praising your pet when it is quiet.

Beg

Begin with your dog in the sit position and hold your dog's toy or titbit just above its nose – you are trying to encourage your dog to shake both its paws at the same time. Reinforce the sit and, with your left hand, try to move the paws up – your right hand holding the toy remains in front of its nose.

Alternatively, ask your dog to sit in front of you placing both of its front legs on you. Hold the toy or titbit just above and in front of its nose and as it balances itself – remove its legs from you.

Remember to say the command "beg" during either method so your pet associates the word with the pose. Praise your dog once they've achieved the position. You will have to try this several times, and it will be easier for small to medium-sized dogs.

Roll Over

Since you have already got your pet to go down on the ground by command (page 31), you are close to being able to get them to roll over. In this trick it is important that your dog is comfortable with being handled all over by you.

Ask your dog to go down. With this achieved, kneel beside your dog and gently roll them over on to their back and onto their other side praising them as they co-operate with you. Saying "roll" or "tummy" as you move your dog over onto its back or side.

You can use a titbit in front of their nose, low on the ground to encourage its participation in this trick. It will take time for your dog to realise that you want them to go over onto their back, and over to the other side. You must remember this is a dominating trick to any dog, as they are exposing their underside to you in a submissive gesture – not all dogs will be happy to comply to your request.

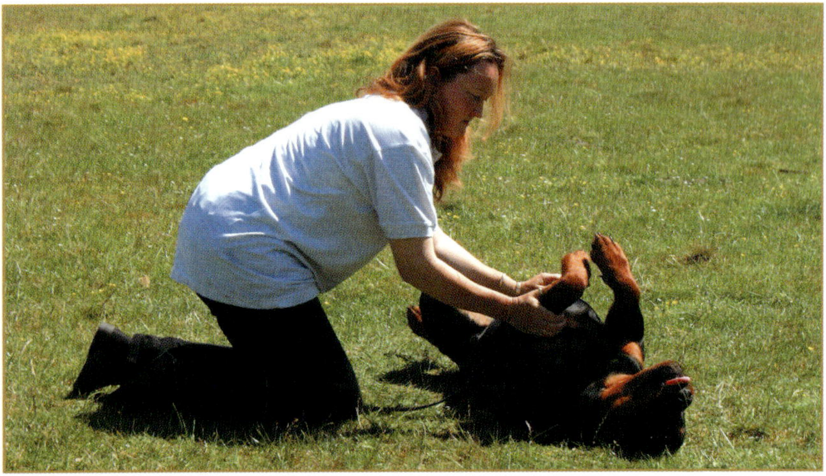

Shake Hands

Your dog should be happy sitting with you for this to work. Once you are in the sit position, kneel or bend down in front of your dog, holding a hidden titbit in your left hand. Gently tap their right paw. (Dogs, like humans can be right or left sided, but in most cases the dog will be right pawed.)

As your pet shifts their weight to give you their paw, praise them and say "shake" giving them the hidden titbit.

Repeat with the left leg once you feel your pet is getting the idea of the trick. Simply add the word left or right to the command, tapping the appropriate paw: "Shake left".

An alternative method is to point to the paw and then say "shake".

Fetch

For your dog to fetch things correctly, they must first be able to hold an object in their mouth. Start with your dog sitting beside you and place a toy in their mouth saying "hold". If necessary, place your hands around their mouth or under their chin to keep their mouth shut. Start by doing this for ten seconds, then increase the time to twenty seconds, then thirty with each session. At the end of each count encourage your puppy or dog to drop the item (explained overleaf).

Praise your dog all the time they are holding the item, so that they realise this is the action you want them to perform.

With the hold command mastered you can progress to teaching your dog or puppy to fetch.

The kindest way of teaching any puppy or adult dog to fetch is by using a soft item, such as a soft toy or knotted T-shirt, and making a game of it.

Play with the item and then throw it a little way for your dog while they are on the lead. Take a couple of steps to go with the dog as encouragement.

Keeping your dog on the lead will ensure the game remains controlled. Without it, your aim of having your dog pick up and return the toy to you can be hard to achieve.

When your dog picks up the article, say "fetch" using an excited voice. Bending over, praise your pet as they comes towards you. Gently take hold of the item in the dog's mouth and ask them to "drop" the article. Praise your dog immediately when they comply.

If you offer a titbit you will find the dog will start to spit the item out before getting it completely back to you, because they cannot eat a titbit with something else in their mouth.

Sometimes it may be necessary to blow on their nose to make them drop the item. If this has to be done, do not offer a titbit, only a verbal praise or pat.

Encourage your dog to take harder items – progress to using an empty kitchen roll centre stuffed with newspaper as a retrieve article – then go on to using a ball which can easily fit into their mouth. After that progress to a plastic or rubber version of the item you wish the dog to retrieve, such as a dog bowl. It is important to make this type of exercise fun for your dog.

Bow and Stand

You will find that your dog naturally assumes this position when waking up after being asleep. So when you see them adopting the position of front down, rear raised, take the opportunity to say "bow". Doing this will lodge in its mind that you like that position and you will be able to work on this trick from there.

Alternatively, to teach your puppy or dog to bow you will need to firstly teach your dog the stand command. Stand in front of your dog with a titbit in your hand, which they can smell, and let them lean into your hand. You should be telling your dog to "stand" as they do this.

Another way to achieve the stand command is to walk, with your dog leaving your left hand free. Ask your dog to "wait", then "stand", placing your left hand near or under their flank to stop it sitting. Give them a little scratch under the tummy area then continue walking saying "come on", then repeat the stand command a few paces on.

From the stand position comes the bow. Ask your dog to stand, using either of the methods just discussed. Place a titbit in your right hand in front of their nose and take it down to the floor between their feet. You might need to move their paws forward so they can achieve the desired position. Your left hand should be stopping its back end from going down on the floor.

This positioning will take several attempts before the dog assumes the desired position, so be patient. Allow your dog to come up and then go through the same procedure a few feet further on.

You need to understand how your breed of dog will assume the position. Some dogs assume the position readily and it will look quite pronounced, others breeds have to be worked into the position gradually.

Crawl

For the crawl to work, your puppy or dog needs to happily accept the down command (page 31).

Begin with the down command, then kneel beside your dog. Place a titbit in front of its nose with your right hand, keep your left hand just above the dog's shoulder blades – should they consider trying to stand up to reach the titbit your left hand will prevent them from rising. Say "crawl' to your pet, and give them encouragement to emphasise what you want them to do.

An alternative way to obtain a crawl is to place a toy or titbit so that to obtain it your dog must crawl under something. However, you should ensure the training obstacle is fairly wide and has ample room for them to be able to pass easily underneath it on their stomach.

Get your dog to perform the down command in front of the obstacle then, by holding the titbit under the obstacle in front of its nose, lure it to follow your right hand by moving it under the object so your dog has to crawl to follow the food, giving the command to crawl as you do so.

Walking on Back Legs

Firstly, it is important for you to understand that there are many large breeds of dog that will be unable to achieve this trick and you should not attempt to train them to do this. Small to medium dogs are best suited to doing this trick well.

It can be taught from the sit, or stand position, whichever your dog is happiest with.

Put a titbit in your right hand, place it above your dog's nose, making sure it is a little higher than usual, so that it will have to jump up a little to obtain it. Say "up" with an excited voice. Keep doing this until you have your dog adopting a standing up position to receive the titbit.

Your dog will find it difficult to balance on two legs, and to maintain its balance to please you it will step forward. This is how the walk is started. Keep your hand in front of your dog's nose with the titbit, moving it forward so that the dog comes to learn to follow the reward in this elevated position.

This exercise is very tiring for your dog and should be done a little at a time. Once you have achieved what you want, stop and try again another day. The best results are gained with repeated exercise over several days.

An alternative method to achieve this trick is to ask your dog to stand up with their paws resting on your legs to obtain a titbit. When they are up on you, walk carefully away backwards helping them to balance with your hand on, or just above, their paws – as you would with a child who is taking its first step.

As always, praise your charge for their efforts, giving them the titbit for the completed task.

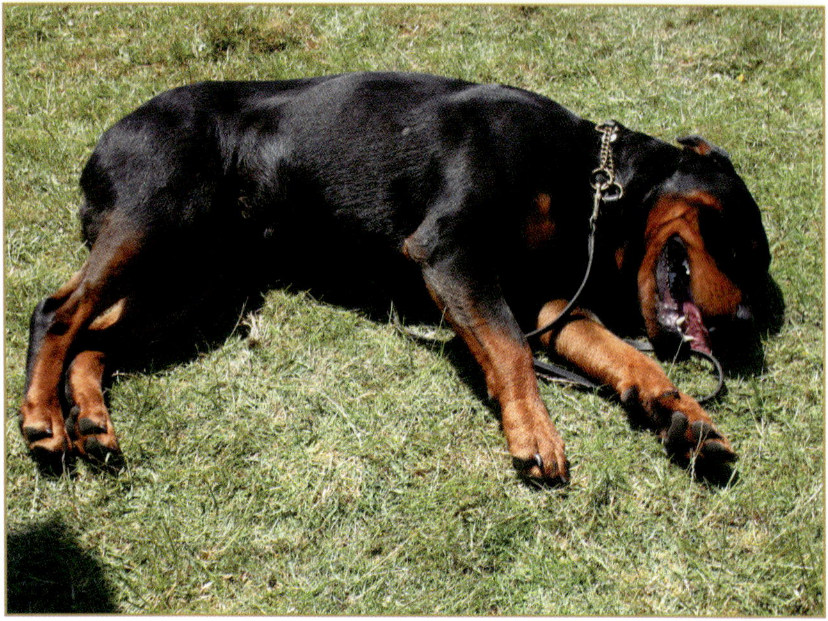

Play Dead

This can be a great deal of fun to teach. Quite simply, pick a moment when your dog is either asleep or just laying flat out on the floor, and give the command, "play dead" or "flat" and praise your dog with a pat if they stay in the position.

Alternatively, ask your puppy or dog to go down next to you, keeping them as calm as possible. Roll your dog gently over onto their side, keeping your hands on the top side of your dog on their body and head.

Say the command "play dead" or "flat" giving only gentle praise (so that they don't get excited) when this is achieved, encouraging your dog to relax and possibly go to sleep.

It is usually easiest to teach this command at the end of a training session when your dog is tired.

It will take several attempts to get your dog to understand that you want them to lie very quietly on the floor.

Do not use titbits in this trick as this will encourage your dog to tense up to receive their reward. Only use gentle praise as your request is complied with – you want your dog to relax rather than get excited.

When you have decided your dog can get up – say "up". Otherwise they will not know how long you want them to stay in that position. More generous praise can be offered once your dog is up and standing.

Balancing Food on the Nose

Please be aware that some breeds of dog, such as the pug, do not have much of a nose to do this with, so it would be very frustrating for you both to attempt it.

You will need to teach your dog to 'leave' before you can complete this trick fully – this means leaving anything, especially food which you have accidentally dropped.

With your dog on the lead, place an item that may interest it a small distance away. As they go to investigate say "leave" and give a firm tug on the lead. This will ensure the dog understands it is not to touch it.

Whenever you see anything that you do not wish your dog to touch you can give the leave command and they will eventually ignore the object. Once this command has been understood, you can go on to balancing food on their nose.

Ask your dog to sit in front of you and in a calm but firm manner show a piece of cheese (semi soft type about the size of a sugar lump).

During training it is unfair to use food that will fall off quickly, making the dog think it has made a mistake, when it is you that has chosen the wrong item. Once you've perfected this trick you can try balancing other foods or even toys on you pet's nose.

Say "leave" and place the cheese cube on their nose. They will look very hard at this item, and you must give them encouragement to make them realise they have done nothing wrong but that by leaving the cheese balancing on their nose they are doing the right thing.

When you remove the cheese just say "thank you" and give the treat to the dog. As with all tricks this will take time to achieve and teach properly, so remain patient spread the training out.

Aerial Tricks

Some dogs, once they can retrieve happily, will be extremely keen on retrieving any article. Dogs that are like this can be successfully made to go on to aerial retrieval. Use an item like a disc, which will fly through the air easily. It is important to use something that will not harm the dog's mouth when they go to take it.

Start by encouraging your dog to jump up to the disc in your hand, holding it about shoulder height, away from your body. Turn in a semi-circle as you hold the disc out. It is important the dog isn't jumping up in one spot – they should be moving as they jump.

When your dog is happy at jumping up to take the disc from your hand, start to throw the disc about 1–2 metres high, and roughly 3–5 metres away. Allow your dog to watch what you are doing while encouraging them to take part.

As you turn and release the disc, give the fetch command. After a few attempts a mid-air retrieval should be accomplished.

Practise by yourself at getting the disc to flow through the air so that your dog will have the best chance to grab the disc mid throw. As you and your dog both get better at the throwing and retrieving, keep adding distance (say a metre at a time) to your throw until you have reached a safe limit.

Ensure you retain control over the throw – don't throw the disc too hard, you need to maintain a constant standard which your dog can become accustomed to.

Some dogs can jump quite high but try to restrain them from jumping to their maximum which could lead to injuries. Larger breeds of dog in particular should not be encouraged to jump high off the ground, as they are more prone to injuries.

Competition Tricks

The following tricks are a step up the dog training ladder. If you have an agility training class nearby it will enable you to get to know the basic groundwork required to make these and other tricks easier. Remember, the dog expects you to know what they are to do.

The skills used in the following tricks are similar to those used in shows and competitions. There are all types of competitions for dogs to compete in. Contact the organisers if you wish to compete – but make sure you and your dog are really ready!

Jumping

Jumping any dog should only be attempted after it has reached eighteen months of age. By this time it is considered that most breeds will have a hardened bone structure that will not be damaged by the extra pressure put on their shoulders from landing, or damage to their hip joints from taking off.

As with any exercise where muscles and ligaments are concerned, the dog should be fit and healthy and have done some exercise before going to activities that require jumping. An overweight dog can do itself a lot of damage, possibly ending up in need of medical attention, so be sensible with your pet.

Don't train on areas that are wet and slippery, find a dry, firm piece of ground. If you can, find a natural jump such as a fallen tree trunk, or you could use an overturned bench. For training purposes it needs to be something you can jump over as well.

Over an Obstacle

Agility dogs perform various tricks that rely on their ability to go over and under obstacles.

Using an overturned bench, begin training by jumping over the obstacle along with your dog. As you jump say to your dog "over". You should both land on the other side without falling or refusing, in which case give a lot of praise to your dog and a well done to yourself. Then have another go. You can repeat this up to a maximum of five times.

Put your dog on a lead and, with an excited voice, show them what you what them to do. Start about two to three metres away from the jump. Aim for your hand holding the lead to be in the centre of the jump at the highest point, and remember, there are two of you jumping.

Over a few lessons, start moving yourself over to the right side, until you have the situation where only your dog is going over the jump. You may find throwing a titbit over the jump will encourage them to go over to get it. Always aim to have the dog go over at the centre of the jump.

With the basics achieved you may then progress to the different types of jumps and develop a hand command so that you may simply point to the jump and your dog will automatically go over it.

Under an Obstacle

To get your dog to go under an obstacle begin, once again, with a bench, a nice wide one that has plenty of clearance for your dog to go under easily.

Since your dog is already enjoying the game of following a toy or titbit, get on your knees next to the bench asking your dog to go under as you throw the toy or titbit under the bench and out the other side.

With the dog on the lead encourage them to go under to reach the toy or titbit. Let go of the lead as your dog goes underneath to reach the treat.

Agility courses often include tunnels so you may wish to increase the size of the obstacle and create a tunnel-like structure with two benches pushed together, or you could use fences to create something similar. Only extend the trick once your dog is ready.

Heel Weaving

This is a fairly easy trick for a well-trained dog that trusts their handler. It comes from the agility dog's routine of weaving through a set line of poles using the command "weave".

To start your dog through your legs you will need to have a loose lead attached to your dog, and a titbit in your right hand.

Lift your left leg up at the knee. Make sure it is right up. Bring your hand underneath your left leg calling your dog "under" or "through".

This is where the dog's trust in you is important. They must be happy to go underneath you as you change legs. With the basic move completed, progress to taking steps.

To start with, take five steps with your dog weaving in and out, increasing by two more steps as you feel your dog is improving, and extending the trick to fifteen steps at the most.

Remember to continuously give the command through or under so the dog is fully aware that this is what you want. The last thing you need is your dog going through your legs when you don't want it to! You can adapt this same technique slightly if want to teach your pet how to weave in and out of poles, the trick performed by agility dogs.

Circling

This can be done with a dog of any size and it is how sheepdogs are trained to go round a flock of sheep, circling either to the left or the right of the flock.

Mastering the fundamentals of weaving and circling will enable your dog to learn more complex agility tricks seen at dog shows. For complete training in these events it will be necessary to seek the help of a professional trainer.

Circling relies heavily on your dog being familiar with the heel command, and you should practise heel work before commencing with this trick.

Holding a toy or titbit in your right hand against your stomach and the lead in your left, start walking forward with your dog following at heel, by the left leg. After a few steps introduce the command "round" to

your dog and encourage the dog to move round in front of you while you continue to walk.

To clarify the intended move, gently tug on the lead bringing it in front of your body. Use the toy or titbit to indicate the direction of the move as well, taking this hand round to the back of the body and swapping hands with the lead so you don't get tangled up. The dog should follow the toy and move around you in a circle.

Continue to say "round" offering encouragement with the toy so that the dog sees it as a game. Remember to keep walking forwards as your dog circles you. If this proves too difficult, practise the command while you remain stationary.

Use the same technique for circling in either direction. It is usual to start training circling to the right before circling to the left.

Conclusion

Training your dog takes patience and a lot of encouragement to be successful. Size and age need not matter when teaching your pet tricks – just remember that you're both meant to enjoy it!

Remember to try again if the trick you are encouraging your pet to do goes wrong. You can always go back to the basic commands and start again.

Give your dog a break from training if things are going wrong – a happy dog will work much better with you than a dog that is continually being told off.

Remember, be firm, be fair and have fun.

Picture Credits

10: Stockbyte. 11: Corel. 12: Elektravision. 17: Royalty-Free/Corbis. 52: Steve Prezant/Corbis. 56: Mark Peterson/Corbis.